Y0-DJP-533

Extreme Scientists

Contents

What to Do

- a dictionary
- a thesaurus
- an atlas

NOW:

- choose a face
- when you see your face, you are the leader
- when you are the leader, follow these steps:

1. Predict

Say to your group:
"I think this page is going to be about..."

You can use these things to help you predict:

- photographs
- captions
- headings
- what you already know

Tell your group to read the page silently.

2. Clarify

When your group has finished reading, ask them if there is anything they don't understand.
Say: *"Is there anything anyone doesn't understand?"*

It could be:
- a word
- something someone has read

3. Ask Questions

Ask your group if anyone would like to ask a question about what they have read.
Say: *"Does anyone have a question they would like to ask?"*

4. Summarize

Now... you can tell your group what the main ideas are on this page.
Say: *"I think this page has been about..."*

Extreme Scientists

I predict this is going to be about...

Extreme scientists are people who work in very difficult and dangerous places. They don't work in laboratories all the time like many other scientists do.

Instead, they search for information that can only be gathered through firsthand experiences.

These scientists might have to go right inside an active volcano or swim with sharks. They may have to explore deep, dark caves, hang from bridges, or dangle from tall trees.

Extreme scientists need to be brave, bold, and daring people. They often risk their own lives trying to get information that could help us in many ways and could even help save the natural world.

STOP

OPINION

Do you think scientists should risk their lives? Why? Why not?

Does anyone need to have anything clarified?

Ice caves in a glacier

Scientists watching a storm

Cave Scientists

Searching for Life in Sulfur Caves

I predict this is going to be about…

Some scientists explore life inside caves. They are called speleologists. Some kinds of caves are more dangerous than others for explorers.

Sulfur caves are full of poisonous gases that can be deadly to people. The acid on the walls can melt flesh. The scientists who go into these caves must wear acid suits and masks that give them oxygen and keep out poisonous gases.

In sulfur caves, there are many animals that cannot be found living anywhere else on Earth. These animals that have adapted to live in this tough environment could hold clues to life on other planets. The environment in a sulfur cave is more like the environment on Mars. Scientists can use the information they gather to learn about what life might be like there.

Does anyone need to have anything clarified?

A cave scientist holding a salamander

Learning Icy Secrets

I predict this is going to be about...

Some cave scientists explore deep ice caves, using ropes to lower themselves into the caves. Once inside the caves, the scientists can study tiny animals and plant life that survive where it is too cold for humans to live. The information the scientists get can be used to help make medicines that may one day cure or even prevent some diseases.

Inside the ice cave, it is like being in a deep freeze. If scientists explore the water in an ice cave, conditions get even more dangerous. Diving in such cold water is very dangerous. Breathing equipment can freeze and the ice is constantly moving. Sharp pieces of ice can break away and fall like spears.

A scientist in Marr Glacier ice cave

Does anyone need to have anything clarified?

Ready to dive

I predict this is going to be about…

Exploring underwater caves is one of the most dangerous and challenging jobs for an extreme scientist. Deep inside the cave it is very dark and damp. Some passages are very narrow, and the scientist may have difficulty squeezing through. There are often many tunnels that stretch for miles, and it would be easy to make a wrong turn.

In the caves there are needle-sharp stalactites and stalagmites that scientists have to be careful not to swim into.

Underwater caves are windows into the past. Explorers have discovered the remains of prehistoric sea creatures. The caves can also provide scientists with clues about how life survives without light, and how some animals adapt to live in different environments.

These cave-diving scientists also map caves where no one has been before to help other divers explore a cave safely.

STOP

When you read, "caves are windows into the past," what picture do you get in your head?

Does anyone need to have anything clarified?

Scientists in Rumbling Volcanoes

I predict this is going to be about...

Some scientists study volcanoes to predict when they are going to erupt and how big an eruption is likely to be. These scientists are called volcanologists.

Volcano science is tricky because volcanoes don't erupt very often, and one eruption may be different from another. A volcanologist uses a seismometer to listen for rumblings deep under the ground, the same way a doctor might listen to a heartbeat with a stethoscope. Sometimes the scientists need to get deep down inside the volcano to take the temperature and to measure the gas pressure. This can help them predict if there is going to be an eruption sometime in the future.

Around the world, millions of people live within the danger zone of an erupting volcano. These extreme scientists have helped to make many people's lives safer.

A helicopter monitors a Mt. Kilauea eruption.

Does anyone need to have anything clarified?

Collecting a sample of hot lava

Volcanologists inside Mt. Pinatubo's caldera

Science on Top of the World

I predict this is going to be about…

Some scientists study the canopy of tall trees in the rain forest. The canopy is difficult to reach, so the risk and challenge for these scientists is getting to the top.

Scientists can use a hunting bow to shoot up a line with a weight on it, over a high branch. Then they are able to climb up the line into the tree. Some scientists study the tops of trees from a gondola on a canopy crane. The gondola can swing in a large circle on the end of the crane arm. This way scientists can study the tops of many trees.

The canopy in a rain forest is very important to scientists. This is where a large percentage of the world's plant and animal species live.

By finding out about life in the canopy, scientists can learn more about it. They can also gain a snapshot of the general health of the rain forest.

Does anyone need to have anything clarified?

A biologist exploring the forest canopy

I predict this is going to be about...

Some scientists who study endangered birds, such as the peregrine falcon, first need to rescue the eggs and the chicks from difficult and dangerous places. These birds sometimes make nests on tall buildings or underneath high bridges. Scientists can find themselves high up on a steel beam, with only a rope holding them, and nothing below them but air and water.

Sometimes angry mother birds swoop in to attack the scientists as they raid the nests.

If scientists didn't find a better place for the birds to live, most would not survive, and the scientists would have nothing to study.

Peregrine chick and mother on a tall building

Does anyone need to have anything clarified?

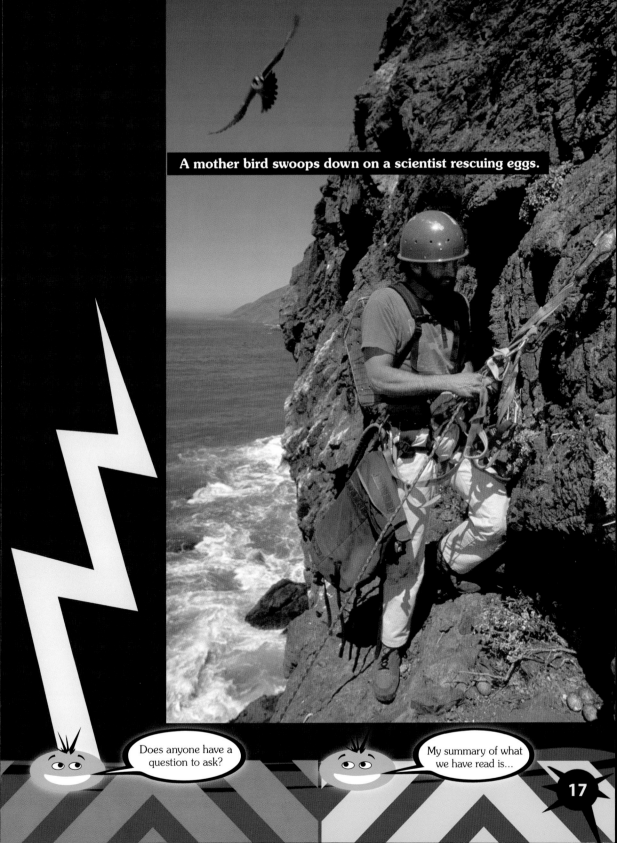

A mother bird swoops down on a scientist rescuing eggs.

Swimming with Sharks

I predict this is going to be about...

The number of great white sharks in the world is getting smaller. Scientists need to study the sharks and find out how many there once were, how many there are now, and how many are needed to make sure they don't become extinct.

Part of the challenge of this job is the fact that great white sharks are one of the most dangerous animals on Earth. Sometimes scientists have to get very close to a shark. The easiest and safest way to do this is from inside a shark cage.

Unfortunately, a shark cage can be dragged to the bottom of the ocean. The scientists can also be trapped in the cage. Sometimes sharks attack the cage. They can shake it, and their razor-sharp teeth can bend the bars.

Some scientists free dive with a shark, to watch how the sharks react to humans without a steel cage.

STOP
OPINION
Do you think that scientists should be trying to save the great white shark? Why? Why not?

Does anyone need to have anything clarified?

18

A diver watching a shark

Teaching the Swans

I predict this is going to be about...

The trumpeter swan is the largest swan in the world, but it was hunted until it nearly became extinct. Because of this, many younger swans have never been taught to migrate by their parents. The swans stay in the place they were born, and don't know what to do during different seasons.

Scientists have to teach the swans how to migrate. One way to do this is to teach the swans to follow an ultralight plane, which they seem to believe is their lead swan.

Another plane, called a chase plane, flies behind the swans. It kind of acts like a sheep dog that is rounding up sheep. The plane darts from side to side, trying to keep the birds together.

The plane is so tiny and light, sometimes swans fly into it and there is not much protection for the pilot.

Does anyone need to have anything clarified?

Trumpeter swans following a plane

Studying Crocodilians

I predict this is going to be about...

The caiman is a crocodilian. It is the largest predator in the Amazon and it is very dangerous. The caiman was nearly hunted to extinction, so the job of extreme scientists is to make sure that caimans don't disappear once and for all.

The scientists work to find out how many caimans there are, and where they go to feed, breed, and nest. The scientists float alongside the caiman in a tiny wooden boat, knowing that at any second the caiman's long jaws could crunch the boat like a soda can. To help get the information they need, the scientists need to mark the caiman with a radio transmitter. This means taking the large, ferocious animal out of the water and onto the land.

Does anyone need to have anything clarified?

Handling a young crocodile

STOP

When you read, "crunch the boat like a soda can," what picture do you get in your head?

Does anyone have a question to ask?

My summary of what we have read is...

Capturing Anacondas

I predict this is going to be about…

The anaconda is one of the biggest snakes in the world, but many have been killed for their skins, and their environments have been destroyed. Scientists are trying to discover where anacondas like to live and breed, and what they prefer to eat.

To capture an anaconda, the scientists walk through the swamp in their bare feet, feeling for the enormous snakes with their toes.

Once an anaconda has been found, the scientists will fight with it until it becomes tired and easier to manage. A radio transmitter can be put on the anaconda, and samples of blood are taken for testing. The more the scientists learn, the more they can do to help protect the anacondas.

Does anyone need to have anything clarified?

The yellow anaconda

Four people hold an anaconda.

Does anyone have a question to ask?

My summary of what we have read is...

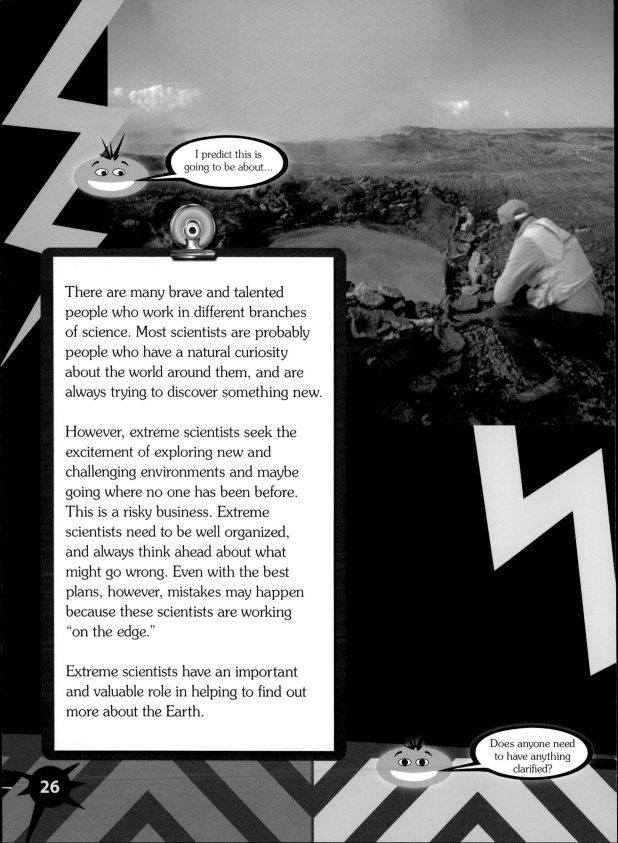

I predict this is going to be about...

There are many brave and talented people who work in different branches of science. Most scientists are probably people who have a natural curiosity about the world around them, and are always trying to discover something new.

However, extreme scientists seek the excitement of exploring new and challenging environments and maybe going where no one has been before. This is a risky business. Extreme scientists need to be well organized, and always think ahead about what might go wrong. Even with the best plans, however, mistakes may happen because these scientists are working "on the edge."

Extreme scientists have an important and valuable role in helping to find out more about the Earth.

Does anyone need to have anything clarified?

A volcanologist taking measurements

Something to Think About

K

What I KNEW
– before reading
the book

L

What I have
LEARNED
– from reading
the book

W

What I WOULD
LIKE to learn
– after reading
the book

Extreme
Scientists

Want to Find Out More?

Try searching in books and on the Internet using these key words to help you:

anacondas
cave scientists
crocodilians
dangerous science
extreme scientists
great white sharks
trumpeter swans
volcanologists

Index